*Presented to:*

Stutsman County Library

in memory of

ADWOLT & RUTH SCOTT

SandCastle 2

Baby Animals

# Piglets

**Kelly Doudna**

ABDO
Publishing Company

Published by SandCastle™, an imprint of ABDO Publishing Company, 4940 Viking Drive, Edina, Minnesota 55435.

Printed in the United States.

Photo credits: Christine Hipkiss/Cordaiy Photo Library Ltd./Corbis, Richard Hamilton Smith/Corbis, The Purcell Team/Corbis, Richard A. Cooke/Corbis, Keren Su/Corbis, Corel, Digital Vision

Library of Congress Cataloging-in-Publication Data

Doudna, Kelly, 1963-
   Piglets / Kelly Doudna.
     p.  cm. -- (Baby animals)
   Summary: Simple text and photographs present the physical characteristics and behavior of piglets.
   ISBN 1-57765-185-5
   1. Piglets--Juvenile literature. [1. Pigs--Infancy. 2. Animals--Infancy.] I. Title. II. Series: Doudna, Kelly, 1963- Baby animals.
SF395.5.D68   1999
636.4'07--dc21                            98-21702
                                                CIP
                                                AC

The SandCastle concept, content, and reading method have been reviewed and approved by a national advisory board including literacy specialists, librarians, elementary school teachers, early childhood education professionals, and parents.

## Let Us Know

After reading the book, SandCastle would like you to tell us your stories about reading. What is your favorite page? Was there something hard that you needed help with? Share the ups and downs of learning to read. We want to hear from you! To get posted on the Abdo Publishing Company Web site, send us email at:

**sandcastle@abdopub.com**

# About SandCastle™

## Nonfiction books for the beginning reader

- Basic concepts of phonics are incorporated with integrated language methods of reading instruction. Most words are short, and phrases, letter sounds, and word sounds are repeated.

- Readability is determined by the number of words in each sentence, the number of characters in each word, and word lists based on curriculum frameworks.

- Full-color photography reinforces word meanings and concepts.

- "Words I Can Read" list at the end of each book teaches basic elements of grammar, helps the reader recognize the words in the text, and builds vocabulary.

- Reading levels are indicated by the number of flags on the castle.

## Look for more SandCastle books in these three reading levels:

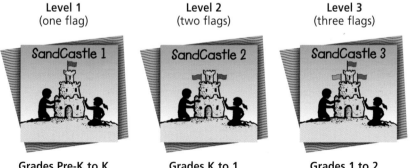

| **Level 1**<br>(one flag) | **Level 2**<br>(two flags) | **Level 3**<br>(three flags) |
|---|---|---|
| **Grades Pre-K to K**<br>5 or fewer words per page | **Grades K to 1**<br>5 to 10 words per page | **Grades 1 to 2**<br>10 to 15 words per page |

A young pig is a piglet.

Piglets live on farms.

Mother pigs are big.

Piglets are small.

Piglets have big ears.

Piglets have flat noses.

Piglets have many brothers and sisters.

Do you?

Piglets like to play
in the mud.

Piglets like to rest on
the cool dirt.

It is fun to play with
a piglet.

This piglet plays
with a kitten.

Who do you play with?

Who are your friends?

# Words I Can Read

## Nouns

A noun is a person, place, or thing

**dirt** (DURT) p. 15
**kitten** (KIT-uhn) p. 19
**mud** (MUHD) p. 13
**pig** (PIG) p. 5
**piglet** (PIG-let) pp. 5, 17, 19

## Plural Nouns

A plural noun is more than one
person, place, or thing

**brothers** (BRUHTH-urz) p. 11
**ears** (IHRZ) p. 9
**farms** (FARMZ) p. 5
**friends** (FRENDZ) p. 21
**noses** (NOHZ-ez) p. 9
**piglets** (PIG-letss)
pp. 5, 7, 9, 11, 13, 15
**pigs** (PIGZ) p. 7
**sisters** (SISS-turz) p. 11

# Verbs
A verb is an action or being word

**are** (AR) pp. 7, 21
**do** (DOO) pp. 11, 21
**have** (HAV) pp. 9, 11
**is** (IZ) pp. 5, 17
**like** (LIKE) pp. 13, 15
**live** (LIV) p. 5
**play** (PLAY) pp. 17, 21
**plays** (PLAYZ) p. 19
**rest** (REST) p. 15

# Adjectives
An adjective describes something

**big** (BIG) pp. 7, 9
**cool** (KOOL) p. 15
**flat** (FLAT) p. 9
**fun** (FUHN) p. 17
**many** (MEN-ee) p. 11
**mother** (MUHTH-ur) p. 7
**small** (SMAWL) p. 7
**young** (YUHNG) p. 5

# Sight Words

farm

kitten

friends